25 Words That Can Change Your Life

The Power To Be Amazing Lies Within You.

Vicky Ford

COPYRIGHT

Copyright © 2016 by Vicky Ford
All rights reserved worldwide.
No part of this publication may be replicated, redistributed, or given away in any form without the prior written consent of the author/publisher or the terms relayed to you herein.
Vicky Ford – Author
This publication is designed to provide accurate and authoritative information in regard to the subject matter covered. It is sold the understanding that the publisher is not engaged in rendering legal, accounting, health or other professional services. If legal advice or other expert assistance is required, the services of a competent professional person should be sought.

Disclaimer
All the material contained in this book is provided for educational and informational purposes only. No responsibility can be taken for any results or outcomes resulting from the use of this material.
While every attempt has been made to provide information that is both accurate and effective, the author does not assume any responsibility for the accuracy or use/misuse of this information.

This book is dedicated
to all those whose
words of wisdom and power
gave me strength, determination, and
Guidance throughout my life,,
especially the lovely
Louise Hay.

May you continue to shine brightly
In our lives..

Table Of Contents

Welcome To
25 Words That Can
Change Your Life.

Book 1

The idea for this series of books came to me as I was reading one of my favorite authors, Louise Hay.

She was one of the modern pioneers when it comes to using affirmations and words in a conscious manner, creating great change in our lives.

Louise passed quietly in September of 2017 and her loving wisdom will be missed.

The ancient Hebrews knew the power of words and wrote their texts accordingly.

We can use words to change ourselves, our lives and other aspects that do not allow us to be our most amazing selves.

We can banish outdated habits, beliefs and negative self talk by using words of power in a conscious way.

25 Words That Can
Change Your Life.

Book 1

How to use this book.

Each word comes with the dictionary meaning and few notes about what this word has meant in my own life or how you might incorporate this word into your life.

I have also included an affirmation for each word inspired by the work of the lovely Louise Hay.

This is a great opportunity to start a journal for each word. This will give you the opportunity to write down your thoughts, affirmations, actions you wish to take or other inspirations that come to you.

You can take each word in turn or go through the book and choose one that may jump out at you saying Pick Me, Pick Me. Let your intuition be your guide.

I hope you enjoy your journey to becoming Your Amazing Self.

If you enjoyed this book please don't keep us a secret. Let your friends know, too.

- *Playfulness* -

Adjective
1. full of play or fun; sportive; frolicsome.
2. pleasantly humorous or jesting:
a playful remark.

- Every day I discover new ways to add a little play to my day.-

Playfulness is one of my favorite Power Words.

Being playful has enriched every aspect of my life as a grownup and has even helped me to heal portions of my past.

Playtime is an important part of childhood, encouraging new ways of learning, connecting with others, laughter, being active.

As we get older many of us leave our playful nature behind as we become involved in more grownup pursuits.

It's time to let your inner child out to play! Blow bubbles, play in the waves, fly a kite, jump in the autumn leave, make snow angels.

It's never to late to add a little play to your day!

My Word For Today Is:

What This Word Means To Me:

My Affirmation or Action For Today:

- *Authenticity* -

Noun
1. the quality of being authentic; genuineness.

- I easily remain authentic and true to myself -

Authenticity can be a tricky one. We are made up of so many elements of personality, aren't we?

We act differently when we are with our friends than we do with our co-workers.

When we are with our children we show different aspects of ourselves than we do with our parents.

And that's OK. I think we can still have authenticity and respect all those different aspects of ourselves. It is what lies at our core that remains authentic.

Those traits that remain constant no matter who we are with.

Our genuine caring, love, connection, and presence is where our authenticity lies.

My Word For Today Is:
____

What This Word Means To Me:
____
____
____
____
____
____
____
____

My Affirmation or Action For Today:
____
____
____

- *Calm* -

1.   free from excitement, agitation or passion;
serenity; tranquil:
2.   a calm face; a calm manner.

- I am calm and peaceful.
I breathe in calm and breathe out Love. -

Being that calm presence during the crazy storms we ride in our daily life can seem an impossible task. We all face stresses that can sometimes feel unbearable.

But each of us is capable of being that calm space. Our day goes more smoothly, our interaction with people brings them ease and diffuses agitation.

Being the calm in the storm does not mean you must stay strong in every situation.

You're not a monk!

You are allowed to lose it every now and then. But you know you will always come back to calm.

My Word For Today Is:
____

____

What This Word Means To Me:
____

____

____

____

____

____

____

____

My Affirmation or Action For Today:
____

____

____

- *Limitless* -

Adjective
1. without limit; boundless:

- I accept that I am a being of limitless Love & Creativity -

Limitless is such an amazing word and can have so much meaning in our lives.

We can have limitless enthusiasm, love, imagination. When we are in the flow of a project that ignites our inner fires, we feel limitless, almost expansive.

When we fall in love we have that same feeling of our love having no boundaries. We just love everything!

And what if, at our very core, we were limitless spiritual beings. Limitless creation, limitless love, limitless potential.

A game changer!

<u>My Word For Today Is:</u>

What This Word Means To Me:

My Affirmation or Action For Today:

- *Kindness* -

> Noun
> 1. the state or quality of being kind :
> 2. kindness to animals.
> 3. a kind act; favor:

*- I easily find many ways to be kind to others
throughout my day -*

Kindness is such a simple act but in a fast paced world it can be forgotten.

Kindness is a conscious act.

It can be as simple as a smile for a stranger, holding the door open for the person behind you or popping a quarter into someone's expired meter.

What is most fun for me is an act of kindness that remains my little secret. As I help another, I also open my own heart and find myself looking for more ways to be kind.

Add a little kindness to your day!

My Word For Today Is:

What This Word Means To Me:

My Affirmation or Action For Today:

- *Capable* -

Adjective
1.having power and ability;
efficient; competent:

-       *I give myself permission to be capable in
all my endeavours.* -

This one's a biggie, folks. There are many instances where I haven't felt capable. It was a scary, disempowering feeling, leading to frustration and fear.

But one day I heard a spiritual speaker say that sometimes we just need permission to feel capable. I realized I wasn't giving myself permission.

What a concept!

Once I started giving myself permission, the doors opened. I was seeing so many ways that I *was* capable which led me to try new things and succeed.

My Word For Today Is:

What This Word Means To Me:

My Affirmation or Action For Today:

- *Personal Power* -

Meaning – To step into one's own power; to take
control of one's situation or life.

*Now is the time for me to step fully into my
Personal Power. -*

Personal Power, to me, means to be strong in who you are...to
own that. Know that you are worthy of choosing your own path,
of being true to yourself.

My own path to Personal Power has had so many twists, turns,
initiations of fear, tears, and finally letting go of who I thought I
was.

At times this journey had me on my knees in complete
surrender. I had to allow space for a higher version of me to
come into being. I set boundaries that represent personal
power for me and honor who I am as a woman and as a human
being.

Through this fire I have discovered I am stronger, smarter, more
courageous and Divine than I ever thought I could be.

My Word For Today Is:

What This Word Means To Me:

My Affirmation or Action For Today:

- *Acceptance* -

Noun

1. The act of consenting to receive.

*- I embrace full acceptance of myself for who I am
in this moment -*

The word acceptance can have so many meanings but in this moment our focus is on accepting who you truly are.

This is the moment where you accept your Divine Self, your highest version of you.

You are perfect, you are more than you know, more than you can perceive and yet you are also so wonderfully human.

Accept that you are an important piece of this puzzle we call life on Planet Earth. You have purpose and uniqueness and just your being here makes a difference.

<u>My Word For Today Is:</u>

What This Word Means To Me:

My Affirmation or Action For Today:

- *Believe* -

> Verb
> To have confidence in the truth, the existence or the reality of something, although without the absolute proof that one is right in doing so.

- I believe in myself, fully and completely -

It may seem controversial but what you believe can shape your reality.

What you believe about yourself, about your life, about the world around you, shapes your experience.

Isn't it wonderful, then, that you can change your beliefs at any time? We don't *have* to believe something if it does not serve us or support us any more. And that's OK.

Our life experience shows us new ways of thinking, giving us an opportunity to evolve and become a higher expression of ourselves.

My Word For Today Is:

What This Word Means To Me:

My Affirmation or Action For Today:

- *Freedom* -

> Noun
> a. The absence of necessity of constraint in choice or action
> b. Liberation from ..... The power of another.

*- My life is my own
and I have the freedom to choose my path. -*

Freedom can be a bit scary. Right? I mean, if you have the freedom to choose how to act, how to think, how to show up in your life, it also means you carry the responsibility of your actions.

And that's awesome! Freedom puts you in the driver's seat. You are free to choose your path, who to love, what to eat, your spiritual beliefs, how you connect with others.

Freedom is a great blessing. Use this gift to create a life that supports your highest vision.

Let your life inspire others to experience freedom in their own lives.

<u>My Word For Today Is:</u>

What This Word Means To Me:

My Affirmation or Action For Today:

- *Boundaries* -

Noun
a. Something that indicates bounds or limits

- I set strong and healthy boundaries for myself -

It took me a long time to understand the idea of boundaries as it applied to me, personally.

For many years I allowed people to treat me in ways that were disrespectful because I did not respect and honor myself. I was afraid people wouldn't like me if I confronted them.

But setting strong, healthy boundaries is all about love; love of yourself. You come first!

You deserve to be treated with respect, you are worthy and once you create your own boundaries, the most amazing people come into your life.

My Word For Today Is:

What This Word Means To Me:

My Affirmation or Action For Today:

- Self-Love -

Noun
The instinct by which ones actions are directed to the
promotion of ones own welfare or well-being.

- I value myself and I am worthy of self-love -

Self-Love is the most important concept there is. When we truly
love ourselves, this love has a wonderful way of spilling over and
touching everything and everyone we touch.

And we must love ourselves first. This is so vital yet we are
afraid. We may feel unworthy, or arrogant or ashamed.

And so I want to say from my heart; you deserve to be loved, you
are worthy of love, it's fun and exciting and wonderful to fall in
love with yourself.

Love yourself first and just let it overflow.

My Word For Today Is:

What This Word Means To Me:

My Affirmation or Action For Today:

- *Integrity* -

Noun
1. Adherence to moral and ethical principles;
soundness of moral character; honesty.

- I live my life with integrity, striving for the best and highest good in all situations. -

Integrity is our moral compass. Without it we are lost. We lose who we are, our wisdom, and our way forward.

Integrity is about having your words match your actions and having those actions come from the heart.

It is wanting the best for all involved, including yourself. It means giving your best, no matter what you are doing.

In life you will come across many who are not in integrity. Stay centered, listen to your heart, know your boundaries and let them go on their way.

My Word For Today Is:

What This Word Means To Me:

My Affirmation or Action For Today:

- *Wisdom* -

Noun
1. The quality of having experience, knowledge and good judgment.

- I have the wisdom that comes, not only from learned knowledge, but from my life experiences and intuition. -

Wisdom, in my mind, is a space of calm and certain knowing. This knowing comes from life experience as much as it does from the active pursuit of knowledge.

Wisdom is also present within that innate inner knowing that comes from listening to the Intuitive aspect of yourself.

I'm sure you have experienced moments of that absolute knowing that something is just right; that there is an absolute truth and certainty in the decision you are about to make.

Learn to trust your own inner wisdom.

My Word For Today Is:

What This Word Means To Me:

My Affirmation or Action For Today:

- *Peace* -

Noun

1. Freedom from disturbance. Quiet and tranquility.

- I have a space within me that is peaceful even when turmoil surrounds me. -

Peace. One of the most powerful concepts we can bring into our lives.

As I make space for Peace in my own heart I notice I am calmer, more balanced and not as reactive.

Life is chaotic but when I focus my mind on actually Being Peace, I find I am much more effective at being whoever I need to be in that moment.

Powerful stuff!! One of the most amazing techniques I use in my own life is also one of the most simple.

Breathe in Peace. Breathe out Love.
Instant Calm.

My Word For Today Is:

What This Word Means To Me:

My Affirmation or Action For Today:

- *Joy* -

Noun
A feeling of great pleasure and happiness.
Delight, rejoicing, elation, bliss.

- Every day I make space in my world for Peace. -

Joy is such a wonderful, life changing word. So simple, yet can give your life more meaning in every moment.

I think Joy, while one of my favorite Life Changing words, can also be the most intangible.

What does Joy look like? What brings me Joy? And how can I do more of that?

Joy has a different meaning for each person and I believe that is part of the wonder of it.

In the wild roller coaster ride we call life, we can find Joy in the moments.

So pause, just be in that moment, within yourself....and find your Joy there.

My Word For Today Is:

What This Word Means To Me:

My Affirmation or Action For Today:

- *Prosperity* -

Noun
A state of being prosperous.
Success, ease of life, good fortune, comfort, security,
wellbeing.

- Prosperity fills my life to overflowing. -

Prosperity, I think, can mean something different to each of us.

For the immigrant who has come from a place of having very little, to having a job that gives them a safe place for their family to live and food to eat, that is prosperity and security.

For others, that feeling of prosperity may never come to them no matter how much they have.

I believe prosperity and gratitude go hand in hand.

Working towards the life you envision, while having gratitude for what you have gives the feeling of prosperity in every moment.

When you already feel prosperous you are open to bringing even more into your life.

<u>My Word For Today Is:</u>

What This Word Means To Me:

My Affirmation or Action For Today:

- *Life* -

Life
1. The condition that separates man and animal from inorganic matter-growth, change,
2. Existence of an individual being - soul

- I love life and life loves me. -

Life is, in itself, a condition filled with change and mystery.

You can breathe life into projects, a venture, a relationship. You can give life by having a child or by planting seeds and nurturing them.

I think we must be conscious of, not only the sacredness of life, but also our participation in life as it pertains to the world around us.

I am aware that when I am in touch with the feeling of vibrant, spirited, passionate life, the world around me responds.

Our planet is filled with life. As we remain connected to this, allowing it to nurture and sustain us, we are a part of that life-giving cycle.

My Word For Today Is:

What This Word Means To Me:

My Affirmation or Action For Today:

- *Sharing* -

Verb
1. To have a portion of something with others
2. To give a portion of something to others.

- What I share comes back to me in wonderful, unexpected ways.
-

Sharing is caring.

 Haven't we all said that as we strive to teach our children this concept as they grow.

As they grow they begin to see a separateness or realization of individuality as they become toddlers; a view that moves from "ours" to "mine and yours". We teach them that sharing can give them happy feelings.

In my own life, I've found, as I share what I have, I love the feeling I get. I share because it feels good for me as well as helps others.

I share hugs and receive love and hugs in return, we support children's causes and know they are being given a better chance in life, we share meals with friends and build strong, supportive relationships.

Share from the heart and magic happens.

My Word For Today Is:

What This Word Means To Me:

My Affirmation or Action For Today:

- *Spirit* -

Noun

1. Nonphysical part of a being. Seat of emotions and character. Harmony of body and soul
2. Qualities of a being, or nation - essence

- I recognize my spirit as a beautiful part of me. -

Spirit: One of my favorite Power Words. Not simply a word but an entire concept that defines our existence on every level of being.

When you see someone across the room and know they are the one....is that not spirit talking to you? This is what happened to my sweetheart and I and we have been happy together for many years.

Spirit, that indefinable aspect of you, is never separated from the whole. It is always connected to all that is.

This is why it is written in ancient manuscripts, we are never alone, never unsupported, even though our ego and physicality fight to have us believe otherwise.

Our Spirit is our greatness, our strength and our empowered selves.

My Word For Today Is:

____

What This Word Means To Me:

____

____

____

____

____

____

____

____

My Affirmation or Action For Today:

____

____

____

- *Friendship* -

Noun
1. A state of being friends, relationship, attachment,

- I have true and lasting friendships. -

Friendship can take on many forms. We have work friendships, social friendships, long distance friendships.....and then there are those friendships that are true, forever relationships that sustain you, enrich you and are truly heart connected.

These are friends that are at your side for the good times and the bad. They have seen your worst side and still love you. They call you out on your own BS and offer help when you are afraid to ask.

It is these friendships that are worth nurturing, for they do require attention but that is the fun part.

Sharing a meal, being there to listen, a crazy day trip for shopping, hiking or just to see what's in the next town are small ways of bringing richness to your friendship.

My Word For Today Is:

What This Word Means To Me:

My Affirmation or Action For Today:

- Connection -

Noun
1. A relationship with a person, place, idea or thing.

- I trust my feeling of connection with my world. -

A connection can be a powerful thing, full of feeling and emotion. Your connection to beliefs and ideals can shape your life and your perception of the world.

A powerful connection to a place you have never been is mysterious and yet, very real.

My first visit to the Island of Kauai was just such an experience. The feeling of being there before, being home and even welcomed by the Island, as though my soul knew this place, was overwhelming.

I believe this was the most powerful kind of connection....that of spiritual knowing that goes beyond what the mind can understand.

And although I have not visited Kauai for several years, that connection remains strong.

My Word For Today Is:

What This Word Means To Me:

My Affirmation or Action For Today:

- *Strength* -

Noun
1. The state of being strong.
2. My word: a state of inner resilience and fortitude.

- I have an inner strength that is unshakable. -

Physical strength is great but it's got nothing on the inner strength of someone who has been through the 'fires of hell' in life and come through it.

I believe those who have recovered from addictions, illness, terrible loss or horrific trauma through accident, abuse, war and natural disaster are the true heroes when it comes to strength.

That strength is a Light that inspires, encourages, motivates and stirs us to action in our own lives.

This is a Light that shines on each of us and allows us to see not only our own strength, but the strength of others.

My Word For Today Is:

What This Word Means To Me:

My Affirmation or Action For Today:

- *Appreciation* -

Noun

I. A recognition of the good qualities of a someone or something.

- In my life I show appreciation for the small things as well as the bigger ones. -

Appreciation is something that, all too often, seems to be lacking in our daily life. We have become so busy we fail to see the many chances we have to show our appreciation.

Whether it is a flower that has fought it's way through concrete to bloom just for you or the young man at his first job bagging your groceries, your appreciation means so much.

It means you stopped, for just a bit, and you were in that moment enough to notice, to be aware, and to say Thank You!

As I write this it is 25 below zero outside. On my way home from the store I saw a rare ice crystal rainbow. I may have been the only person to notice it. I hope not.

But I'm full of appreciation for this lovely act of nature that blessed my day.

My Word For Today Is:

What This Word Means To Me:

My Affirmation or Action For Today:

- *Wonder* -

Noun
I. Feeling of surprise mixed with admiration, caused
by something beautiful, unexpected, unexplainable

- My life is filled with wonder. -

Do you still feel that childlike sense of wonder as you journey
through your life?

I hope you do. I think a sense of wonder, about amazing selves,
our life, our world, the cosmos, adds such a sense of fun and
curiosity to our lives.

How boring it would be if nothing about life excited us or
inspired us to want to know more.

I feel wonder as I see marriages that work so well despite
hardships. I feel wonder at how children learn, how incredible
flowers smell, or look at the millions of stars in the sky, knowing
I am a part of it all.

I feel wonder when I realize we are all amazing beings sharing
this incredible journey together.

My Word For Today Is:

What This Word Means To Me:

My Affirmation or Action For Today:

Hello everyone.

I hope you have enjoyed your journey through your 25 Words That Can Change Your Life book and journal.

These are the words that have inspired me, healed me, encouraged me and molded me into who I am today. And I'm not done yet!

In short, these are just some of the words that have changed my life.

At different times in my life I have needed to focus on courage, on playfulness, on boundaries, on gratitude and so much more.

I wrote this book because I really wanted to help others. Life can be tough and sometimes people just need to know there is someone who helps them believe, just for a moment, that they are amazing.

 I want to share what life has taught me, how I made it through the challenges, and how I 'evolved' from who I was to who I am now. This book is just part of what has worked for me on this crazy carnival ride we call life.

If this book has helped you on your path in some small way, I am grateful.

Bless you on your life's journey. Please don't keep us a secret. If this little book helped you we would be so happy if you would share it around to your friends and those you feel might have some fun with it.

Thank you so much.

Now go out into the world and be your Amazing Self!

Vicky M. Ford

Hello. I hope you enjoyed the first book in this series
25 Words Than Can Change Your Life.

I would love to know how it may have helped you in your life.

You can connect with me here:

https://www.facebook.com/vickyfordbooks/
http://vickyfordbooks.com/
https://twitter.com/beachgypsy8
https://www.pinterest.com/beachgypsy9/

Check out the other books I have available on Amazon:

Don't keep us a secret. Spread the word and
remember....

Add a Little Play to Your Day!

Check out our other great books from Dancing Tree Publishing